The Funniest Football Quotes

Humorous Quotations for All Sports Fans

James Conrad

CONTENTS

INTRODUCTION

This is a book for those who love football and all that goes with it. Many of us will have played in football teams where people have said something amusing, something exquisitely stupid or just plain embarrassing. It is part of the enjoyment of football that these experiences are shared with teammates and competitors.

The collection of quotes assembled here are basically is essentially the similar experiences of the great and the good of football

FOOTBALL MATHS

You need at least eight or nine men in a ten-man wall.
Mark Lawrenson

When you are 4-0 up you should never lose 7-1.
Lawrie McMenemy, Southampton manager

We must have had 99% of the game. It was the other 3% that cost us the match.
Ruud Gullit

I've had 14 bookings this season—eight of which were my fault, but seven of which were disputable.
Paul Gascoigne

Leicester were 5,000 – 1 to win the League but ended up as champions. What are the odds of that happening?
Neil Lennon

Statistics are there to be broken.
Chris Kamara

We are three games without defeat is another way of looking at it. But if we are honest we have taken two points from nine.
Kevin Keegan

The Germans only have one player under 22, and he's 23.
Kevin Keegan.

For Burnley to win they are going to have to score.
Chris Kamara

I would not be bothered if we lost every game as long as we won the league.
Mark Viduka

They were numerically outnumbered
Gary Birtles

Whichever team scores more goals usually wins.
Michael Owen

Can you believe it? James Beatty has it on the 18 yard line – 22 yards out.
Chris Kamara

My heart has only one colour: white and blue.
João Pinto

They're the second best team in the world, and there's no higher praise than that.
Kevin Keegan

With Harry, two plus two always makes five, not three.
Milan Mandaric

Newcastle, of course, unbeaten in their last five wins.
Brian Moore

Maths is totally done differently to what I was teached when I was at school.
David Beckham

Ritchie has now scored 11 goals, exactly double the number he scored last season.
Alan Parry

Four minutes to go... four long minutes... three-hundred and sixty seconds.
Alistair Alexander

Chile have three options : they could win or they could lose.
Kevin Keegan

I am a firm believer that if you score one goal the other team have to score two to win.
Howard Wilkinson

On another night they'd have won 2-2.
Ron Atkinson

There's only one place you want to be and that's Wembley, Old Trafford or Anfield.
Mick Channon

The 2,000 away fans will be unhappy. In fact half of them have gone. There's only 500 left.
Chris Waddle

In their last four Blackburn have lost 3-0, 3-1, 5-3 and 3-2. It doesn't take a rocket scientist to work out that's 12 goals conceded.
Alan Brazil

Bolton have won just three of their last two games.
Ian Abrahams

Is it offside? We are talking milliliters.
Steve McManaman

There's only one person gets you sacked and that's the fans.
Paul Merson

If you don't concede any goals you'll win more games than you lose.
Wayne Bridge

There's still 45 minutes to go - for both sides, I would guess.
Brian Marwood

Karl Henry's been sent off for a deliberate red card.
Chris Kamara

It was six of a half and one dozen of the other.
Danny Higginbotham, Chester City

THE PERSON IN THE MIDDLE

I never comment on referees, and I'm not gonna break the habit of a lifetime for that prat.
Ron Atkinson

Referees, like most of us, are human beings.
Piara Power, Chief Executive of Football against Racism

It's like a toaster, in the ref's shirt pocket. Every time there's a tackle, up pops a yellow card.
Kevin Keegan

I think the fact that Sir Alex Ferguson rested Howard Webb had a lot to do with the result.
Noel Gallagher after City's 6-1 defeat of United at Old Trafford

It was like the referee had a brand-new yellow card and wanted to see if it worked.
Richard Rufus

He's had three offside decisions, two right, two wrong.
Chris Kamara

It was lucky that the linesman wasn't stood in front of me as I would have poked him with a stick to make sure he was awake.
Ian Holloway

The ref was booking so many I thought he was filling his lotto numbers.
Ian Wright

After the match an official asked for two players to take a dope test. I offered the ref.
Tommy Docherty

If he fouls you he normally picks you up but the referee doesn't see what he picks you up by.
Ryan Giggs on Dennis Wise

McCarthy shakes his head in agreement with the referee.
Martin Tyler

The ref was vertically 15 yards away.
Kevin Keegan

You can say the linesman's scored. It was a goal coming from the moon or from the Anfield Road stands.
Jose Mourinho

A highly contagious decision.
Neil Mellor

Football wasn't meant to be run by linesmen and air traffic control.
Tommy Docherty

Can you believe that? A female linesman. Women don't know the offside rule.
Andy Gray

If there is a foul, you have to fall. I call it 'helping the referee to make a decision'. That's not cheating.
Jose Mourinho

The linesman flagged initially, because he thought I was an Oldham player. Fair enough, I did have a replica shirt on ... but I also have a big furry head.
Chaddy The Owl, the Oldham mascot, who was surprised to be given offside during a match.

I shouldn't really say what I feel, but Poll was their best midfielder in the goal. You saw him coming off at half-time and at the end. He smiled so much, he obviously enjoyed that performance. I think the referee should be banned.

Neil Warnock

David Elleray was that far away he would have needed binoculars. I really think it's about time we use the means to sort these things out rather than relying on some bald-headed bloke standing 50 yards away.

Neil Warnock

If that was a penalty, I'll plait sawdust.

Ron Atkinson

The Media

I've got nothing to say. Any questions?
Ray Hudson, Miami Fusion manager

Reporter: What is your impression of Jermaine Pennant?
Gordon Strachan: I don't do impressions.

Interviewer: Who was the biggest influence on your career?
Jimmy Greaves: Vladimir Smirnoff.

Reporter: Are you enjoying your time in Blackpool, Ian?
Ian Holloway: I love Blackpool. We're very similar. We both look better in the dark.

Jimmy Hill: Don't sit on the fence Terry, what chance do you think Germany has got of getting through?
Terry Venables: I think it's fifty - fifty.

Reporter: Gordon, can we have a quick word please?
Gordon Strachan: Velocity

Reporter: What would you be if you weren't a footballer?"
Peter Crouch: Probably a virgin

Anne Robinson: In the equation E = MC², devised by Einstein, what does the letter E stand for?
Gascoigne: Er...elephant

Jeff Stelling: There's been a red card but for who Chris Kamara?
Chris Kamara: I don't know Jeff has there? I must have missed that. Is it a red card? I don't know, I don't know the rain must have got in my eyes Jeff. No you're right I saw him go off but I thought they were bringing a sub on Jeff. Still nil nil ha ha ha

Reporter: Gordon, do you think James Beattie deserves to be in the England squad?"
Gordon Strachan: I don't care, I'm Scottish.

Reporter: How's (Hasney) Aljofree's injury?
Ian Holloway: Hasney's bust his hooter. He can smell round corners now.

Richard Keys : Well Roy, do you think that you'll have to finish above Manchester United to win the league ?

Roy Evans: You have to finish above everyone to win the league Richard.

Reporter: Welcome to Southampton Football Club. Do you think you are the right man to turn things around?

Gordon Strachan: No. I was asked if I thought I was the right man for the job and I said: 'No, I think they should have got George Graham because I'm useless'.

Reporter: There's no negative vibes or negative feelings here?

Gordon Strachan: Apart from yourself, we're all quite positive round here. I'm going to whack you over the head with a big stick. Down negative man, down.

Ian St. John: Is he speaking to you yet?

Jimmy Greaves: Not yet, but I hope to be incommunicado with him in a very short time.

Reporter: Ian, have you got any injury worries?
Ian Holloway: No, I'm fully fit, thank you.

Reporter: So, Gordon, in what areas do you think Middlesbrough were better than you today?
Gordon Strachan: What areas? Mainly that big green one out there...

Reporter: So, Gordon, any plans for Europe this year?
Gordon Strachan: Aye, me and the wife quite fancy Spain in August.

Reporter: This might sound like a daft question, but you'll be happy to get your first win under your belt, won't you?
Gordon Strachan: You're right. It is a daft question. I'm not even going to bother answering that one. It is a daft question, you're spot on there.

The Sun: Which player was the worst trainer you have seen?
Dave Savage: Mark Kennedy used to bring a cigar and deckchair into training.

Reporter: Is that your best start to a season?
Gordon Strachan: Well I've still got a job so it's far better than the Coventry one, that's for sure.

Reporter: You don't take losing lightly, do you Gordon?
Gordon Strachan: I don't take stupid comments lightly either.

Gary Lineker: So, Gordon, if you were English, what formation would you play?
Gordon Strachan: If I was English I'd top myself.

Reporter: So, Gordon, any changes then?
Gordon Strachan: Naw, still 5ft 6", ginger and a big nose.

John Sinclair : Will Steve Agnew take this free kick just outside the box?
Steve Agnew : I'm sitting next to you, so I don't think it'll be me.

I have nothing, nothing to say. Nothing, nothing to say. Nothing to say, I have nothing to say. Nothing to say, I am so sorry, I have nothing to say.
Jose Mourinho

Reporter: David, was Wayne Rooney disappointed to lose his youngest goal scorer record on Monday to the young Swiss striker?
David Beckham: No, but I'm sure it'll just make him even more determined to get it back against Portugal tonight.

Callum McManaman: I always believed we'd win it.
Interviewer: How does it feel?
Callum McManaman: I can't believe it.

Don't tell those coming in the final result of that fantastic match, but let's just have another look at Italy's winning goal.
David Coleman

If you closed your eyes, you couldn't tell the difference between the two sides.
Phil Brown

Sorry, but I've had a really busy day today. I've been playing in a charity golf day to raise money for a boy who was seriously injured in a car accident. I've had to drive like a lunatic to get here.
Ray Houghton on Talksport Radio.

Sporting Lisbon in their green and white hoops, looking like a team of zebras.

Peter Jones, commentator

I've always said that there is a place for the press but they haven't dug it yet.

Tommy Docherty

That's football, Mike, Northern Ireland have had several chances and haven't scored but England have had no chances and scored twice.

Trevor Brooking

I've just watched the replay and there is absolutely no doubt: it's inconclusive.

Garth Crooks

Chelsea fans will have switched off their televisions and be listening to their radios with their hands over their ears biting their nails.

Alan Green

He's just got the Midas touch right now. Everything he touches turns to silver.

Richard Keys

The way Arsenal are passing the ball is as if they are telepathetic.
Graham Taylor

Beckham is no rocket surgeon.
Paddy O'Connell, Radio 4

I've got my doubts, there's no doubt about it.
Alan Brazil

Our talking point this morning is George Best, his liver transplant and the booze culture in football. Don't forget – the best caller wins a crate of John Smith's bitter.
Alan Brazil, Talk Radio

Tense and nervous are not the words, though they are the words
Chris Kamara

In the end, Rosicky initially did well.
Andy Townsend.

After Chelsea scored, Bolton epitulated.
Paul Merson

One accusation you can't throw at me is that I've always done my best.
Alan Shearer

It's now 1-1, an exact reversal of the score on Saturday.
Radio 5 Live

Nobody cares if Le Saux is gay or not. It is the fact that he openly admits to reading the Guardian that makes him the most reviled man in football.
Piers Morgan

England have not won a game for three months. The fact that we have not played one is irrelevant. Graham Taylor should hang, and so should his successor.
Item in Viz, September 1993.

The Opposition

In football everything is complicated by the presence of the opposition.
Jean-Paul Sartre

Wayne Rooney has a man's body on a teenage head.
George Graham

If Everton were playing at the bottom of the garden, I'd pull the curtains.
Bill Shankly

I was guest speaker at Sunderland's end of season dinner. That was in October.
Tommy Docherty

We didn't underestimate them. They were just a lot better than we thought.
Sir Bobby Robson

The difference between Everton and the Queen Mary is that Everton carry more passengers.
Bill Shankly

I know this is a sad occasion, but I think that Dixie would be amazed to know that even in death he could draw a bigger crowd to Goodison than Everton on a Saturday afternoon.
Bill Shankly speaking at the funeral of Everton legend Dixie Dean.

When I've nothing better to do, I look down the league table to see how Everton are getting along.
Bill Shankly

Anybody who can do anything in Leicester but make a jumper has got to be a genius.
Brian Clough, referring to ex player Martin O'Neil's success at Leicester.

A lot of football success is in the mind. You must believe you are the best and then make sure that you are. In my time at Anfield we always said we had the best two teams on Merseyside, Liverpool and Liverpool reserves.
Bill Shankly

I tried to watch the Tottenham match on television in my hotel yesterday, but I fell asleep.
Arsene Wenger

It's always great fun getting attacked. One of the highlights of my career. The fella who beat me up got fined £100 for that, but they had a whip-round in the pub and he got £200.

Gordon Strachan, discussing being attacked by a Celtic fan when playing for Aberdeen in 1980

England have the best fans in the world and Scotland's are also second to none.

Kevin Keegan

There are three types of Oxo cubes. Light brown for chicken stock, dark brown for beef stock and light blue for laughing stock.

Tommy Docherty discussing Manchester City

No one wants to grow up and be a Gary Neville.

Jamie Carragher

I went into the Chelsea dressing room to swap shirts and it was bigger than my house.

Dickson Etuhu, Norwich

As we went out on the pitch, he handed me a piece of paper. It was the evening menu for the Liverpool Royal Infirmary.

Jimmy Greaves about Tommy Smith

PLAYERS

He covers every blade of grass out there... but that's only because his first touch is so crap.
Dave Jones on Carlton Palmer

Viv Anderson has pissed a fatness test.
John Helm

The lance had to be boiled.
John Terry

If you'd been at school, he would have been the boy who ate worms.
Neil Ruddock on Stan Collymore

Football was my only hope in life. I wasn't too good at school. To give you an idea, I managed to fail art in a class where my uncle was the teacher.
Richarlison

He looks like he is pulling an old fridge.
Mark Lawrenson on Mertesacker

Sam was a ball playing defender. If he wasn't with the ball, he was playing with your balls.
Dave Bassett

As a boy I was torn between being a footballer or joining a circus. At Partick Thistle I did both.
Alan Hansen

I've told the players we need to win so that I can have the cash to buy some new ones.
Chris Turner, Peterborough's manager before a Cup match

In 1969 I gave up women and alcohol. It was the worst 20 minutes of my life.
George Best

Titus looks like Tyson when he strips off in the dressing-room, except he doesn't bite and has a great tackle.
Sir Bobby Robson on Titus Bramble.

People will look at Bowyer and Woodgate and say 'Well, there's no mud without flames'.
Gordon Taylor

It's not fair to say Lee Bowyer's a racist. He'd stamp on anyone's head.
Rodney Marsh

I'd compare myself to Zinedine Zidane – a humble guy who just happened to be the best.
Anelka

Oh, he had an eternity to play that ball, but he took too long over it.
Martin Tyler

Without being too harsh on David Beckham, he cost us the match.
Ian Wright

They say I slept with seven Miss Worlds. I didn't. It was only four. I didn't turn up for the other three.
George Best

Beckham? His wife can't sing and his barber can't cut hair.
Brian Clough

He's had a lovely career for the talent he's got.
David Pleat on Peter Crouch

At Rangers I was third choice left back behind an amputee and a Catholic.
Craig Brown

I've got more important things to think about. I've got a yogurt to finish by today, the expiry date is today. That can be my priority rather than Agustin Delgado.

Gordon Strachan

I only wanted him for the reserves anyway.

Bill Shankly, To the players after failing to sign Lou Macari

Dumbarton player Steve McCahill has limped off with a badly cut forehead.

Dave Bassett

I was in for 10 hours and had 40 pints - beating my previous record by 20 minutes.

George Best, after having a blood transfusion after a liver transplant

If a player is not interfering with play or seeking to gain an advantage, then he should be.

Bill Shankly

The ugliest player I ever signed was Kenny Burns.

Brian Clough

I used to go missing a lot... Miss Canada, Miss United Kingdom, Miss World.
George Best

I always used to put my right boot on first, and then obviously my right sock.
Barry Venison

I definitely want Brooklyn to be christened, but I don't know into what religion yet.
David Beckham

Is the Pope Catholic. No I'm serious. I really need to know.
David Beckham

I've been consistent in patches this season.
Theo Walcott

Sandro's holding his face. You can tell from that it's a knee injury.
Dion Dublin

What can I say about Peter Shilton? Peter Shilton is Peter Shilton, and he has been Peter Shilton since the year dot.
Sir Bobby Robson

I'm not saying he's pale and thin, but the maid in our hotel room pulled back the sheets and remade the bed without realising he was still in it.

Brian Clough, in reference to former Notts Forest player Brian Rice

It's an incredible rise to stardom. At 17 you're more likely to get a call from Michael Jackson than Sven Goran Eriksson.

Gordon Strachan

Veggard Heggem, my word, he must have a Yamaha down his shorts.

Terry Butcher

I was a bit anxious when I got to the stadium, but in all fairness if hadn't been anxious I'd have been worried.

Paul Robinson, Leeds

Hartson's got more previous than Jack the Ripper.

Harry Redknapp talking about striker John Hartson.

They compare Steve McManaman to Steve Heighway and he's nothing like him, but I can see why – because he's a bit different.

Kevin Keegan

It took a lot of bottle for Tony to own up.

Ian Wright, on Tony Adam's confession to alcoholism

I wasn't surprised that Nic wanted to take Chelsea's offer. We were only paying him two dead frogs and a conker.

Gary Megson, Bolton

He reminds me of a completely different version of Robbie Earle.

Mark Lawrenson

Gary Speed has never played better, never looked fitter, never been older.

Sir Bobby Robson

What do you think of Manchester United's three Rs - Rooney, Ronaldo and van Nistelrooy?

Rob McCaffrey

Michael Owen is irreplaceable, but Sven has Emile Heskey, James Beattie, Wayne Rooney and Darius Vassell and whoever he picks can do the job.
David Platt

If I had a blank piece of paper there'd be five names on it.
Kevin Keegan

That's a yellow card for Cazoria. So, the next time he's involved in Europe, he won't be.
George Hamilton, RTE commentator

I'll tell you what my real dream is. I mean my absolute number one dream that will mean I die a happy man if it happens. I want to see a UFO. They're real. I don't care if you look at me like that. UFOs are a definite fact and I've got to see one.
Paul Gascoigne

I once said Gazza's IQ was less than his shirt number and he asked me: 'What's an IQ?'
George Best

Danny Welbeck is unique. He reminds me very much of Darius Vassell.

John Barnes

Somebody compared him to Billy McNeil, but I don't remember Billy being crap.

Tommy Docherty

I've stopped drinking, but only while I'm asleep.

George Best

I might go to Alcoholics Anonymous, but I think it would be difficult for me to remain anonymous.

George Best

There's no point in asking me. I can't remember what happened last night.

George Best, when asked 'What happened next?' on A Question of Sport.

I'm so glad there will now be two good-looking guys at Real. I've felt so lonely in such an ugly team.

Roberto Carlos on news that Beckham ad signed with Real Madrid

It's all very well batting from the same hymn sheet.
Charlie Nicolas

Celtic jerseys are not for second best, they don't shrink to fit inferior players.
Jock Stein

What a shot. That's completely unstoppable, but the goalkeeper has got to do better for me.
Michael Owen

I was surprised but I always say nothing surprises me in football.
Les Fedinand

He was a player that hasn't had to use his legs even when he was nineteen years of age because his first two yards were in his head.
Glenn Hoddle

Today's top players only want to play in London or for Manchester United. That's what happened when I tried to sign Alan Shearer and he went to Blackburn.
Graeme Souness

None of the player are wearing earrings. Kjeldberg, with his contact lenses is the closest we can get.

John Motson

I don't want to be playing in the Under 21s forever.

David Bentley

The trouble is he is a pony without a trick.

Brian Clough

I'd been ill and hadn't trained for a week and I'd been out of the team for three weeks before that, so I wasn't sharp. I got cramp before half-time as well. But I'm not one to make excuses.

Clinton Morrison

If you look at the last ten games and you turn the league table upside down, we wouldn't be far off top six.

Stephen Hunt

I am never one to make excuses but I couldn't see the ball because the floodlights were in my eyes.

Damien Duff

Simon Tracey has got the brains of a rocking horse.
Dave Basset assessing his Sheff Utd goalkeeper

Jordan Henderson is a player who likes to do his business in the middle of the park.
Jason McAteer

I blew the lot on vodka and tonic, gambling and fags. Looking back, I think I overdid it on the tonic.
Stan Bowles

If only he could pass a betting shop like he does a football.
Reg Drury, journalist, on Stan Bowles

You need 15 players of that elk and keep them together.
Bobby Gould

Gary Neville was captain, and now Ryan Giggs has taken on the mantelpiece.
Rio Ferdinand

(Shaun) Derry would insist on being sick before every game. By which I mean, if the nerves hadn't made him naturally sick, he would stick his fingers down his throat. At the risk of stating the obvious, it really killed the Portsmouth dressing room vibe.

Peter Crouch

If I played for Scotland my grandma would be the proudest woman in the country, if she wasn't dead.

Mark Crossley

Wisey said I think too much. But I have to do all his thinking for him.

Gianfranco Zola discussing Dennis Wise

GEOGRAPHY

I'd like to play for an Italian club, like Barcelona.
Mark Draper

Romania are more Portuguese than German.
Barry Venison

Do you remember when we played in Spain in the Anglo-Italian?
Shaun Newton

It was like living in a foreign country.
Ian Rush on his move to Juventus

Playing with wingers is more effective against European sides like Brazil than English sides like Wales.
Ron Greenwood.

If I was still at Ipswich, I wouldn't be where I am today.
Dalian Atkinson

In terms of the Richter scale this defeat was a force 8 gale.
John Lyall

I don't want Rooney to leave these shores but if he does, I think he'll go abroad.
Ian Wright

2-0 is a cricket score in Italy.
Alan Parry

Welcome to Bologna on Capital Gold for England versus San Marino with Tennent's Pilsner, brewed with Czechoslovakian yeast for that extra Pilsner taste and England are one down.
Jonathan Pearce

It's going to be difficult for me – I've never had to learn a language and now I do.
David Beckham on his move to Spain

Argentina won't be at Euro 2020 because they're from South America.
Kevin Keegan

All the sheep in this country and there is no bacon.
Paul Gascoigne on a New Zealand hotel

All the cul-de-sacs are closed for Scotland.
Joe Jordan

The Belgians will play like their fellow Scandinavians, Denmark and Sweden.
Andy Townsend

I'm amazed to find those countries are in Europe.
Tony Pulis after the Europa League draw sent Stoke to Turkey, Ukraine and Israel

I told him Newcastle was nearer to London than Middlesbrough, and he believed me.
Kevin Keegan signing Rob Lee

What I saw in Holland and Germany was that the majority of people are Dutch in Holland and German in Germany.
Peter Taylor

THE FUTURE

If history repeats itself, I should think we can expect the same thing again.
Terry Venables

I know what is around the corner - I just don't know where the corner is.
Kevin Keegan

Predictions are only for after the game.
João Domingos Pinto

Will I become a coach in the future? No way, I'd never be able to put up with someone like me.
Romario

That was in the past - we're in the future now.
David Beckham

I'm going to make a prediction - it could go either way
Ron Atkinson

Our team was on the edge of a cliff, but we managed to get our act together and take a step forward.

Joao Pinto

If we start counting our chickens before they hatch, they won't lay any eggs in the basket.

Sir Bobby Robson

I can never predict my future because a big part of my future is already behind me.

Guus Hiddink

This could be a repeat of what will happen in the European games next week.

David Coleman

I came in 11 years ago. I remember it like it was tomorrow.

David Moyes

Apparently, when you head a football, you lose brain cells, but it doesn't bother me. I'm a horse. No one's proved it yet have they?

David May

England can end the millennium as it started - as the greatest football nation in the world.
Kevin Keegan

There'll be no siestas in Madrid tonight.
Kevin Keegan

I never make predictions and never will.
Paul Gascoigne

There is nobody fitter at his age, except maybe Raquel Welch.
Ron Atkinson

I don't believe in superstitions. I just do certain things because I'm scared in case something will happen if I don't do them.
Michael Owen

We are a young side that will only get younger.
Paul Hart

I am sure David and Alex will sit down and decide who should be the predecessor to his job.
Paul Ince

You'd need medusa to predict that.
Charlie Nicholas

Football's all about yesterday, it's all about now.

Paul Merson

SKILLS OF THE GAME

Football is a game of skill, we kicked them a bit and they kicked us a bit.

Graham Roberts.

They used to say that if I'd shot John Lennon, he would still be alive today.

Gary Birtles

When he sold you a dummy you had to pay to get back in the ground.

Jim Baxter on Chelsea winger Charlie Cooke

Wilkins sends an inch perfect pass to no one in particular.

Byron Butler

Footballers these days often have to use their feet.

Michael Owen

Carlton Palmer can trap the ball further than I can kick it.

Ron Atkinson

One of his strengths is not heading.
Kevin Keegan

Phil Neville was treading on dangerous water there.
Ron Atkinson

I've seen some recently who could trap a ball further than I could kick it. When they pass it, they should attach this message: 'To whom it may concern' And they're getting 50 grand a week and upwards.
Tommy Docherty

He was in the right place at the right time, but he might have been elsewhere on a different afternoon.
Tony Gubba

It's not nice going into the supermarket and the woman at the till is thinking "dodgy keeper".
David James

He dribbles a lot and the opposition don't like it - you can see it all over their faces.
Ron Atkinson

Never go for a 50-50 ball unless you're 80-20 sure of winning it.

Ian Darke.

The Spaniards have been reduced to aiming aimless balls into the box.

Ron Atkinson

I've never scored a goal in my life without getting a pass from someone else.

Abby Wambach

Well, Clive, it's all about the two M's—movement and positioning.

Ron Atkinson

I hear Glenn Hoddle has found God, that must have been one hell of a pass.

Jasper Carrott

We had a word with him about diving and since then the lad's come on leaps and bounds.

Billy Dodds

Julian Dicks is everywhere. It's like they've got eleven Dicks on the field.

Radio commentator

Keith Gillespie just lacks a little bit of inconsistency.
Graeme Le Saux

He's using his strength and that is his strength, his strength.
Kevin Keegan

He is an interesting player - short back legs.
David Pleat

Chris Waddle is off the pitch at the moment – exactly the position he is at his most menacing.
Gerald Sinstadt

Sometimes he does the brilliant things really well.
Lee Sharpe

Michael Owen – he's got the legs of a salmon.
Craig Brown

He was probably one of the worst players I've ever seen. He once said to me: 'I'm good in the air.' I replied: 'So was Douglas Bader.'
Tommy Docherty on Jimmy Hill

I'd like to have seen Tony Morley left on as a down-and-out winger.
Jimmy Armfield

Now that is defying the laws of gravity.
Harry Neal, referring to a goal from an acute angle

Nicky Butt, he's another aptly named player. He joins things, brings one sentence to an end and starts another.
Barry Davies

Ian Rush is deadly ten times out of ten, but that wasn't one of them.
Peter Jones

Poor Scott Carson. Just two more hands and another chest and he would have saved it.
Jimmy Greaves

He is a goal scorer, not a natural born one - not yet. That takes time.
Glenn Hoddle

Can Messi be suspended for acting? Barcelona is a cultural city with many great theatres and this boy has learned very well. He's learned play-acting.

Jose Mourinho

Our strikers couldn't score in a brothel.

Tommy Docherty

We've got great speed in the team, not just Gary Speed, but great speed.

Sir Bobby Robson

There was nothing wrong with his timing. He was just a bit late.

Mark Bright

Your pace is deceptive son. You're even slower than you look.

Tommy Docherty to Leighton James

We need a big, ugly defender. If we had one of them, we'd have dealt with County's first goal by taking out the ball, the player and the first three rows of seats in the stands.

Ian Holloway

Judging by the shape of his face, he must have headed a lot of goals.

Harry Redknapp on Iain Dowie

Once Tony Daley opens his legs you've got a problem.

Howard Wilkinson

There are some real positives for Wales. Their back four's not bad, sometimes.

Iain Dowie

FOREIGN PLAYERS

If you've got three Scots in your side, you've got a chance of winning something. If you've got any more, you're in trouble.
Bill Shankly

Samassi Abou don't speak the English too good.
Harry Redknapp

Djimi Traore had to adapt to the English game, and he did that by going out on loan to Lens last season.
Ian Rush

Mancini's got that Italian style, the old joie de vivre.
Perry Groves, pundit

What's a geriatric? A German footballer scoring three goals.
Bob Monkhouse

If you said as much as "how are you" to him (Rosicky), he would then be injured for two and a half months.
Emmanuel Adebayor

Mkhitaryan fits us like an arse on a bucket. What he offers is exactly what we need.
Jurgen Klopp

I bet their dressing room will smell of garlic rather than liniment over the next few months.
Brian Clough. On the number of French players in the Arsenal team

When he was carried off at Leicester someone asked me if he was unconscious, but I didn't have a clue. He's always like that.
Gordon Strachan on Claus Lundekvam

Germany are a very difficult team to play. They had 11 internationals out there today.
Steve Lomas

His first touch is like a trampoline. He's not going to make it.
Andy Keogh on Usain Bolt's chances

If people had seen me walking on water, you can be sure someone, somewhere would have complained: 'Look at that Berti Vogts, he can't even swim'.
Berti Vogts

I think that France, Germany, Spain, Holland and England will join Brazil in the semi-finals.
Pele

At last England have appointed a manager who speaks English better than the players.
Brian Clough, discussing the appointment of Sven Goran Eriksson as England manager

I could win the league with Olympiacos. They've won it 107 times and it's only been going 106 years. Why has it always got to be a foreign manager? What does he know about the Premier League?
Paul Merson on Marco Silva

Javier Chevanton don't speak the language too good.
Kevin Bond

Henning Berg, one of the players classified as a foreigner, which obviously as a Norwegian is something he's used to.
Radio commentator

If Glenn Hoddle had been any other nationality, he would have had 70 or 80 caps for England.
John Barnes

It's a huge honour to wear number 7 at Liverpool. I think about the legends; Dalglish, Keegan and that Australian guy.
Luis Suarez not remembering Harry Kewell

I don't think there is anybody bigger or smaller than Maradona.
Kevin Keegan

A real Irish football fan is one who knows the nationality of every player on the Republic of Ireland team.
Jack Charlton

I dreamt of playing for a club like Manchester United, and now here I am at Liverpool.
Sander Westerveld

My history's not very good, but did David win?
Andy Gray

There is no precedent for what Suarez did, other than he's done it before.
Danny Mills

The news for Nigeria is that they're two-nil down very early in the game.
Kevin Keegan

It was like he was being controlled by a 10 year-old on a PlayStation.
Gary Neville on David Luiz

If you pay them the wages they'll come. We all kid ourselves: "I've wanted to play for Tottenham since I was two, I had pictures of Jimmy Greaves on my wall." It's a load of bull. Here's £80,000 a week. Lovely jubbly.
Harry Redknapp on overseas players

Ireland need fresh impotence.
Phil Babb

Fabregas literally carries 10 yards of space around in his shorts.
Ray Wilkins

I had no idea who my teammates at Genoa were when I signed. So, I turned on my PlayStation and looked them up on FIFA.

Krzysztof Piątek

Torres scored three but other than that I kept him pretty quiet.

Michael Duberry

Before my Besiktas debut they sacrificed a lamb on the pitch and daubed its blood on my forehead for luck. They never did that at QPR.

Les Ferdinand

He's six foot something, fit as a flea, good looking – he's got to have something wrong with him. Hopefully he's hung like a hamster – That would make us all feel better. Having said that, me missus has got a pet hamster at home, and his cock's massive.

Ian Holloway discussing Ronaldo

Didier Drogba had malaria, so he's not 100% fit for whatever reason.

Glenn Hoddle

PHILOSOPHY

Amongst all unimportant subjects, football is by far the most important.
Pope John Paul II

Football's football; if that weren't the case it wouldn't be the game it is.
Garth Crooks

Football: a sport that bears the same relation to education that bullfighting does to agriculture.
Elbert Hubbard

International football is the continuation of war by other means.
George Orwell

In football the worst blindness is only seeing the ball.
Nelson Rodrigues

Football is all very well as a game for rough girls, but it is hardly suitable for delicate boys.
Oscar Wilde

When the seagulls follow the trawler, it is because they think sardines will be thrown into the sea.
Eric Cantona

If a Frenchman goes on about seagulls, trawlers and sardines, he's called a philosopher. I'd just be called a short Scottish bum talking crap.
Gordon Strachan

We managed to wrong a few rights.
Kevin Keegan

Football is like fighting a gorilla. You don't stop when you are tired. You stop when the gorilla is tired.
Chris Coleman

Football is the ballet of the masses.
Dmitri Shostakovich

Some people believe football is a matter of life and death, I am very disappointed with that attitude. I can assure you it is much, much more important than that.
Bill Shankly

I'm not a believer in luck but I do believe you need it.
Alan Ball

Football is like chess, but without dices.
Lukas Podolski

Most of the people who can remember when we were a great club are dead.
Notts County chairman.

Women should in the kitchen, the discotheque and the boutique, but not in football.
Ron Atkinson

It's an unprecedented precedent.
Clark Carlisle

If you don't believe you can win, there is no point in getting out of bed at the end of the day.
Neville Southall

I can see the carrot at the end of the tunnel.
Stuart Pearce

If you stand still there's only one way to go, and that's backwards.
Peter Shilton

A football team is like a piano. You need eight men to carry it and three who can play the damn thing.
Bill Shankly

If God had wanted us to play football in the clouds, he'd have put grass up there.
Brian Clough discussing long ball football

Hate doesn't belong on the pitch. Such emotions should be acted out together with your wife in the living room.
Berti Vogts

The problem at Wimbledon seems to be that the club has suffered a loss of complacency.
Joe Kinnear

If you need just a first eleven and four others, why did Columbus sail to India to discover America?
Claudio Ranieri

The unthinkable is not something we are thinking about at the moment.
Peter Kenyon

It all went a bit grape-shaped.
Jason McAteer

Tony Fernandes is in that goldfish bowl and he's swimming against the tide.
Niall Quinn

The silence is getting louder.
Dave Woods

We need to realise we're now the head of the mouse, and not the tail of the lion. It's a Spanish expression.
Rafa Benitez

The ball is round, the game lasts ninety minutes, and everything else is just theory.
Sepp Herberger

Sometimes you see beautiful people with no brains. Sometimes you have ugly people who are intelligent, like scientists.
Jose Mourinho

If we played like this every week we wouldn't be so inconsistent
Bryan Robson

I don't mind Roy Keane making £60,000 a week. I was making the same when I was playing. The only difference was I was printing my own.
Mickey Thomas, former Man United player and convicted of counterfeiting

There's too much – I don't know what the word is – scientology in the game.
David Pleat

The biggest thrill of my life was being at my son's birth. I was there because I was suspended.
Razor Ruddock

People call it Armageddon, but I think it is worse than that.
Terry Butcher

We gained more from the game than they did... except they got the points.
Brian Little

The Beautiful Game

It really is an amazing result; 0-0 at half time.
Chris Kamara

I don't have any tattoos, but that's mainly because none of my limbs are wide enough to support a visible image.
Peter Crouch

I said to my wife 'Come on it's Valentine's Night, I will take you out somewhere special'. So, I took her to Brentford against Southend.
Alan Curbishley

Our season is not beyond our wildest dreams – because they usually involve Elle Mcpherson.
Paul Duffen, Hull Chairman

I don't see the problem with footballers taking their shirts off after scoring a goal? They enjoy it and the young ladies enjoy it too. I suppose that's one of the main reasons women come to football games, to see the young men take their shirts off. Of course, they'd have to go and watch another game because my lads are as ugly as sin.
Ian Holloway

Is Dreamcast the name of the team?
Prince Philip on seeing an Arsenal sponsor's logo

Darlington will become the most successful club in England.
George Reynolds

I do go to football sometimes, but I don't know the offside rule or free-kicks - or side kicks - or whatever they're called.
Victoria Beckham

Look, there's no rule in soccer against biting your opponent. There's not even a rule against eating your opponent. The only rule in soccer is that you can't use your hands.
Luis Suarez

I lost my balance, making my body unstable and falling on top of my opponent. At that moment I hit my face against the player leaving a small bruise on my cheek and a strong pain in my teeth.
Luis Suarez

Sometimes the pendulum swings both ways.
Kevin Keegan

I'd rather play in front of a full house than an empty crowd.
Johnny Giles

Everything's been really positive and smooth. Apart from, obviously, the season.
David Beckham

Women's football does have its knockers.
Adrian Durham

The rules of soccer are very simple, basically it is this: if it moves, kick it. If it doesn't move, kick it until it does.
Phil Woosnam

Hodge scored for Forest after 22 seconds - totally against the run of play.
Peter Lorenzo

I couldn't be more chuffed if I were a badger at the start of the mating season.
Ian Holloway after QPR beat Cardiff

We're halfway round the Grand National course with many hurdles to clear. So, let's make sure we keep our feet firmly on the ground.
Mike Bailey, Charlton manager

We deserved to win this game after hammering them 0-0 in the first half.
Kevin Keegan

Merseyside derbies usually last 90 minutes and I'm sure todays won't be any different"
Trevor Brooking

Strangely, in slow motion replay, the ball seemed to hang in the air for even longer
David Acfield

Giroud scored a brilliant header with the last kick of the game.
Chris Kamara

Football today, it's like a game of chess. It's all about money.
Newcastle United Fan, Radio 5 Live

We lost because we didn't win.
Ronaldo

We beat them four nil and they were lucky to get nil.
Bill Shankly

He will be called Ronald, because we like going to McDonald's.
Ronaldo on his baby

It's end to end stuff, but from side to side.
Trevor Brooking

I've been at Port Vale for 16 years. Even the Great Train Robbers didn't get that long a sentence.
John Rudge

Both sides have scored a couple of goals, and both sides have conceded a couple of goals.
Peter With

Not to win is guttering.
Mark Noble

And with 4 minutes gone, the score is already 0-0.
Ian Dark

For those of you watching in black and white, Spurs are in the all-yellow strip.
John Motson

A game is not won until it is lost.
David Pleat

Everything in our favour was against us.
Danny Blanchflower

When they don't score they hardly ever win.
Michael Owen

Of course, I didn't take my wife to see Rochdale as
an anniversary present. It was her birthday.
Would I have got married in the football season?
Anyway, it was Rochdale reserves.
Bill Shankly

In the first-half we were like the Dog and Duck, in
the second-half we were like Real Madrid. We
can't go on like that. At full-time I was at them
like an irritated jack russell .
Ian Holloway

The beauty of Cup football is that Jack always has
a chance of beating Goliath.
Terry Butcher.

The match will be shown on Match of the Day later this evening and if you don't want to know the result look away now as we show you Tony Adams lifting the cup for Arsenal.
Steve Rider

If we'd kept a clean sheet tonight, we'd have won 1-0.
Steve Cotterill, after a 2-1 defeat

Villa will probably play a lot worse than this and lose.
Alan Parry

If I had been born ugly, you would have never heard of Pelé.
George Best

It is typical of me to be finishing a long and distinguished drinking career just as the government is planning to open pubs 24 hours a day.
George Best

We'll have more football later. Meanwhile, here are the highlights from the Scottish Cup final.
Gary Newbon

Manchester United could only beat Exeter 2-0 –
and it was just 1-0 at one point.
Alan Brazil

Yes, yes, I know all the jokes. What else could I
have expected at Highbury? But I went to Chelsea
and to Tottenham and to Rangers, and saw the
same thing: that the natural state of a football fan
is bitter disappointment, no matter what the
score.
Nick Hornby

Aston Villa are seventh in the league. That's
almost as high as you can get without being one
of the top six.
Ian Payne

There's such a fine line between defeat and
losing.
Gary Newbon

Players prefer the FA Cup because it's the end of
season curtain-raiser.
Peter With

Poland nil, England nil, though England are now looking the better value for their nil.
Barry Davies

Southampton have beaten Brighton 3-1. That's a repeat of last year's result when Southampton won 5-1.
Des Lynam

The first half has gone how I almost half-anticipated.
Jimmy Armfield

That showed a total lack of disrespect from the player.
Garth Crooks

My wife doesn't like football . One day she called me 10 minutes before a game to find out where I was.
Peter Crouch.

I've still got my old school report. It says I was dyslexic, backward, mentally deficient and illiterate. I have all the qualifications you need to be a football club chairman.
Doncaster chairman George Reynolds

TACTICS

The area you're trying to protect at corners is the goal.
Chris Kamara

If it's going to go wrong, I want it to go wrong the way I want it to.
John Hughes, manager

Today was about our lack of ability to not produce the ability we've got.
Sam Allardyce

If you can't outplay the opposition, you must outnumber them.
Terry Venables

You can't play with a one-armed goalkeeper...not at this level.
Kevin Keegan

If it stays as it is I can't see it altering.
Graham Taylor

I've got passion but no idea of tactics. I'd be like a black Kevin Keegan.
Ian Wright

I just wanted to give my players some technical advice. I told them the game had started.
Ron Atkinson

We're in a no-win situation, except if we win we'll go through to the next round.
Graeme Le Saux

It's real end to end stuff, but unfortunately it is all at Forest's end.
Chris Kamara

The tide is very much in our court now.
Kevin Keegan

Manchester City are defending like beavers.
Chris Kamara

Barnsley have started the way they mean to begin.
Chris Kamara

If you're a burglar, it's no good poncing about outside somebody's house, looking good with your swag bag ready. Just get in there, burgle them and come out. I don't advocate that obviously, it's just an analogy.

Ian Holloway, explaining his attacking tactics

The first ninety minutes of a football match are the most important.

Sir Bobby Robson

Gary always weighed up his options especially when he had no choice.

Kevin Keegan

Football is simple. You are in time or too late. When you are too late, you should start sooner.

Johan Cruyff

Statistics are like mini skirts, they give you lots of good ideas, but hide what's important.

Ebbe Skovdahl, Aberdeen manager

I'd love to be a mole on the wall in the Liverpool dressing room at half-time.

Kevin Keegan

Football is a simple game; 22 men chase a ball for 90 minutes and at the end, the Germans win.
Gary Lineker

I was saying the other day, how often the most vulnerable area for goalies is between their legs.
Andy Gray

I'm not religious. In Spain all 22 players make the sign of the cross before they enter the pitch. If it works all matches must therefore end in a draw.
Johan Cruyff

You don't want to be giving away free kicks in the penalty area.
Ron Atkinson

You can't do better than go away from home and get a draw.
Kevin Keegan

There was nothing wrong with the performance, apart from throwing away the game.
Glenn Hoddle

He wears a suit, so he is a tactician. He wears a tracksuit, so he is a motivator. He carries a clipboard, so he is a bus conductor.

Stuart Pierce analyzing Rafa Beintez

When you finish playing football young man, which is going to be very soon, I feel you'll make a very good security guard.

David Pleat to a 17 year old Razor Ruddock

MANAGERS

I promise results, not promises.
John Bond

They brought on someone who cost more than our stadium.
Brendan Rodgers, Swansea manager, on City's Sergio Aguero

The nice aspect about football is that, if things go wrong, it's the manager who gets the blame.
Gary Lineker

When I first became a manager, with Dunstable, attendances were so low we used to tell the team the crowd changes.
Barry Fry

The important thing is he shook hands with us over the phone.
Alan Ball

Matt (Busby) was the eternal optimist. In 1968 he still hoped that Glenn Miller was just missing.
Pat Crerand

There will have to be a bubonic plague for me to pick Di Canio.
Italy coach Giovanni Trapattoni

We can't behave like crocodiles and cry over spilt milk and broken eggs.
Giovanni Trappatoni, Italian manager

You can't say my team aren't winners. They've proved that by finishing fourth, third and second in the last three years.
Gerard Houllier.

Please don't call me arrogant, but I'm the European Champion and I think I'm the special one.
Jose Mourinho

I didn't say them things that I said.
Glenn Hoddle

People ask me what makes a great manager and I say it is good players. Crap players get you the sack, it's as simple as that.
Tommy Docherty

Mind you, I've been here during the bad times too - one year we came second.
Bob Paisley

Very few of us have any idea whatsoever of what life is like living in a goldfish bowl, except of course a goldfish.
Graham Taylor

We have money for sardines and I'm thinking lobster. I will do my best to try and bring in the best players. I will look to the lobsters and sea bass, but if not we must buy sardines. But sometimes the sardines can win games.
Carlos Carvalhal, Swansea manager

Alex McLeish just had his hands in his head.
Chris Kamara

Allegations are all very well, but I would like to know who these alligators are.
Ron Saunders.

Tell him he's Pele and that he's playing up front for the last 10 minutes.
John Lambie to the physio as his striker recovers from concussion

I'm out at the moment, but should you be the chairman of Barcelona, AC Milan or Real Madrid, I'll get straight back to you. The rest can wait.
Joe Kinnear's answerphone message while at Wimbledon

Telling a player to get his hair cut counts as coaching as far as I'm concerned.
Brian Clough

For all his horses, knighthoods and championships, he hasn't got two of what I've got. And I don't mean balls.
Brian Clough. This is a reference to Sir Alex Ferguson's failure to win two successive European Cups.

I wish Glenn luck but he is putting his head in the frying pan.
Ossie Ardiles assessing Glenn Hoddles' chances of retaining the England post

If Roman Abramovich helped me out in training we would be bottom of the league and if I had to work in his world of big business, we would be bankrupt.
Jose Mourinho

I wouldn't say I was the best manager in the business. But I was in the top one.
Brian Clough

I was feeling as sick as the proverbial donkey.
Mick McCarthy

Ah yes, Frank Sinatra. He met me once y'know?
Brian Clough

Alex Ferguson is the best manager I've ever had at this level. Well, he's the only manager I've actually had at this level. But he's the best manager I've ever had.
David Beckham

The River Trent is lovely, I know because I have walked on it for 18 years.
Brian Clough

When you give success to stupid people, it makes them more stupid sometimes and not more intelligent.
Arsene Wenger

We talk about it for 20 minutes and then we decide I was right.

Brian Clough on discussing players opinions

The minute's silence was immaculate, I have never heard a minute's silence like that.

Kevin Keegan

Rome wasn't built in a day. But I wasn't on that particular job.

Brian Clough

To be second with one game to go – you can't ask for more.

Stuart McCall

The only way we will get into Europe is by ferry.

Kevin Keegan

I am in a good position at the moment because no-one is running the club. I am hoping there is nobody out there to sack me.

Stuart Murdoch, Wimbledon manager

If they made a film of my life, I think they should get George Clooney to play me. He's a fantastic actor and my wife thinks he would be ideal.
Jose Mourinho

I had mixed feelings. Like watching my mother-in-law drive over a cliff in my car.
Terry Venables

There are two types of manager. Those who've been sacked and those who will be sacked in the future.
Howard Wilkinson

Football hooligans – well, there are 92 club chairmen for a start.
Brian Clough

The transfer market's so dead I've been phoning myself and disguising my voice for a bit of interest.
Gerry Francis

Everyone's got tough games coming up. Manchester United have got Arsenal, Arsenal have got Manchester United and Leeds have got Leeds.
Sir Bobby Robson

I said to the lads at halftime, I said, there was nothing to say.
Sir Bobby Robson

The problem with being a manager is it's like trying to build an aircraft while it is flying.
Brendan Rogers

I was on a drip in a hospital bed and this player came in to see me. I thought he was was enquiring about my health. He never even asked how I was. All he was interested in was how he stood regarding the contract. He'd even bought his agent in.
John McClelland, St Johnstone manager

In my teams, when we win, we all win, and when we lose, I lose.
Jose Mourinho

There is no pressure at the top. The pressure is being second or third.
Jose Mourinho

It was Milan and Prada or Sunderland and Primark.
Steve Bruce, Sunderland manager, on his efforts to sign David Beckham

When Rioch came to Millwall we were depressed and miserable. He's done a brilliant job of turning it all around. Now we're miserable and depressed."
Danny Baker

I would have given my right arm to be a pianist.
Sir Bobby Robson

No regrets. None at all. My only regret is that we went out on penalties. That's my only regret but no, no regrets.
Mick McCarthy

The boys' performance was so good that I've run out of expletives to describe it.
Micky Mellon, Fleetwood Town manager

Cloughie called me Edward. I told him I preferred Teddie. He said 'Right you are Edward'.

Teddy Sheringham

When I played for Dundee the manager was Bob Shankley, Bill's brother. I should have sensed the worst when he started positioning players for the team photograph and told me 'Just sit at the end of the row son. A pair of scissors will get rid of you'.

Craig Brown

I just opened the trophy cabinet. Two Japanese soldiers came out.

Tommy Docherty when Wolves manager

We don't use a stopwatch for our Golden Goal competition. We use a calendar.

Tommy Docherty at Wolves again

I told Posh fans I'd get them out of Division Two when I arrived as manager. I did, by taking them straight into Division Three

Barry Fry

Kristine's out shopping as usual. I'm down the Job Centre looking for employment. Funny old game innit?

Barry Fry answerphone message after getting the sack from Birmingham

Some parts of the England managers job I did very well, but not the key part of getting players to win football games.

Kevin Keegan

Arsenal didn't have one single chance, including the goal.

Avram Grant

The wife told me it looked as if I knew what I was doing a bit more.

Gareth Southgate on swapping a tracksuit for a suit.

Every dog has its day, and today is woof day! Today I just want to bark!

Ian Holloway after gaining promotion to the Championship

You weigh up the pros and cons and try and put them in chronological order.

Dave Bassett

Although we are playing Russian roulette we are obviously playing catch – 22 at the moment, and it's a difficult scenario to get my head round.
Paul Sturrock

I never succeeded in bringing to the field what was going on in my brain. I had the talent for the fifth division, and the mind for the Bundesliga. The result was a career in the second division.
Klopp said.

I knew my England career was never going to get off the mark again when manager Graham Taylor kept calling my Tony. That's my dad's name.
Mark Hateley

ZLATAN

Reporter: What did you get your wife for her birthday?
Zlatan: I got her nothing, she already has Zlatan.

Zlatan: Only God knows who will go through.
Reporter: It's hard to ask him.
Zlatan: You're talking to him.

I can't help but laugh at how perfect I am.
Zlatan

First I went left, he did too. Then I went right, and he did too. Then I went left again, and he went to buy a hot dog.
Zlatan

An injured Zlatan is a serious thing for any team.
Zlatan

They're lucky I didn't come 10 years ago because I would be the president today.
Zlatan on playing in MLS

I came like a king, left like a legend.
Zlatan, on his leaving PSG

Give them a bicycle with my autograph and that will be enough.
Zlatan and his idea for the payment of female footballers

A World Cup without me is nothing to watch, so it is not worth waiting for the World Cup.
Zlatan

Swedish style? No. Yugoslavian style? Of course not. It has to be Zlatan-style.
Zlatan

Arsene Wenger asked me to have a trial with Arsenal when I was 17. I turned it down. Zlatan doesn't do auditions
Zlatan

When you buy me, you are buying a Ferrari. If you drive a Ferrari you put premium petrol in the tank, you hit the motorway and you step on the gas. [Pep] Guardiola filled up with diesel and took a spin in the countryside. He should have bought a Fiat.
Zlatan

I like Balotelli: he's even crazier than me. He can score a winner, then set fire to the hotel.

Zlatan

ONE LAST THING...

If you have enjoyed this book I would love you to write a review of the book on Amazon. It is really useful feedback as well as giving untold encouragement to the author.

Many thanks

James Conrad

Printed in Great Britain
by Amazon

15586125R00058